# VULTURES

Rourke Enterprises, Inc.
Vero Beach, Florida 32964

PHOTO CREDITS

All Photos by the Author


ACKNOWLEDGMENTS

The author wishes to thank the following for
photographic assistance in the preparation of this
book: Busch Gardens/The Dark Continent, Tampa,
Fla.; Chicago Zoological Society (Brookfield Zoo);
San Diego Wild Animal Park; Florida's Weeki
Wachee; Mike Wells; Joan Daniels; Linda Elbert;
Joel Edelstein; Greg Sorini; Bonnie Georgiades;
Judee Roney


**Library of Congress Cataloging-in-Publication Data**

Stone, Lynn M.
  Vultures / by Lynn M. Stone

    p. cm. — (Bird discovery library)
  Includes index.
    Summary: Describes the appearance, habits, nesting, infancy,
feeding, and importance to humans of this bird of prey.
    ISBN 0-86592-324-8
    1. Vultures—Juvenile literature. [1. Vultures.] I. Title.
  II. Series: Stone, Lynn M. Bird discovery library.
  QL696.F33S77 1989                    88-30196
  598'.912 - dc19                         CIP
                                                AC

2

Lappet-faced Vulture
*(Torgos tracheliotus)* of Africa

# TABLE OF CONTENTS

# VULTURES

Vultures are big, usually bare-headed birds with sharp, hooked beaks. They are related to hawks and eagles. Vultures, hawks, and eagles are all **birds of prey** which hunt during the day.

Most birds of prey use their sharp, strong toes, called **talons,** to kill other animals for food. The animals that they eat are their **prey.**

Vultures have talons, but they are not very powerful. They are more useful for walking than for grasping prey. Also, vultures do not fly very fast, so they rarely try to kill animals. Instead, vultures feed upon dead animals.

Black Vulture
(Coragyps atratus) Eating Fish

# WHERE THEY LIVE

There are over 20 **species,** or separate kinds, of vultures. They live on every continent except Australia and Antarctica. The two largest American vultures are called condors.

Vultures prefer dry, open places where it is easy for them to see dead animals.

Seven species of vultures live in North America and South America. Of these, three species can be found in the United States. The black vulture *(Coragyps atratus)* lives in the South and Southwest. The turkey vulture *(Cathartes aura)* lives throughout the United States and in southern Canada. (Many Americans refer to vultures as "buzzards.")

Until recently a third species lived in California. It was the California condor *(Gymnogyps californianus).* Now the California condor is found only in zoos.

Black and Turkey Vultures
*(Cathartes aura)* Soaring

## HOW THEY LOOK

Vultures are generally black, brown, or brown and white. A vulture's head may be orange, pink, white, black, or red. The South American king vulture's *(Sarcoramphus papa)* head looks like a rainbow!

At rest, a vulture looks much like a hawk or eagle except for its hunched shoulders and bare head. In flight, a vulture's wings are long and wide. They are ideal for **soaring** high in the sky. A condor's wings, from tip to tip, may stretch 10 feet.

The bearded vulture *(Gypaetus barbatus)* of Europe and Asia is the most handsome of the group. Unlike other vultures, the bearded vulture has head feathers. This vulture sometimes eats bones. It doesn't need a bare head because it is not as likely to poke its head into **decaying** flesh as the other vultures.

Bearded Vulture
*(Gypaetus barbatus)*
of Europe, Asia, and Africa

# THE VULTURE'S BARE HEAD

For most vultures, head feathers would just get in the way. A vulture often pokes its head into dead animals, and the bird's head becomes bloody. Because skin cleans more easily than bloodstained features, vultures' heads are bare.

The featherless head also helps the vulture avoid disease, which it might catch from decaying animals. Sunlight kills many of the germs that settle on the vulture's bare head.

For a vulture, the naked head is like a name tag. A red-headed vulture in the United States has to be a turkey vulture. A vulture with a black head is a black vulture.

Turkey Vulture

Egyptian Vulture
(*Neophron percnopterus*),
Young Adult; of Europe,
Africa, and Asia

Hooded Vulture
(*Necrosyrtes monachus*)
of Africa

## THE VULTURE'S DAY

Vultures, with wings outstretched, like to sun themselves in the early morning. Later, they flap upward from their perches and begin to hunt.

Vultures spend much of their day ''on the job.'' A vulture's job in nature is to help clean up. That makes the vulture a **scavenger,** an animal that feeds on dead animals.

Vultures often hunt in flocks. Looking for dead animals, they soar to great heights and travel long distances.

The dead animals are called **carrion.** Vultures generally find carrion by using their keen eyes. The turkey vulture, however, may also use a fine sense of smell.

Turkey Vulture

# THE VULTURE'S NEST

Most of the vultures of Europe, Asia, and Africa build nests of sticks in trees. Up to 12 African white-backed vultures *(Pseudogyps africanus)* may nest in one tree.

None of the seven species of American vultures actually builds a nest. The five smaller vultures of North America and South America lay their eggs on the ground. The condors lay eggs on rocky cliffs.

Most species of vultures lay two eggs. Andean *(Vultur gryphus)* and California condors lay only one egg, and they don't nest every year. That is part of the reason that condors have become **endangered** animals. Condors are in danger of disappearing forever.

African White-backed Vulture
*(pseudogyps africanus)*

# BABY VULTURES

Baby vultures stay at the nesting place when they hatch. Their parents cough up soft food for them to eat.

Some species of vultures grow up much faster than others. A turkey vulture can fly from its nesting place about nine weeks after it hatches. Young condors, however, depend upon their parents for nearly a year! By then, the young condor is as large as the parents. A condor will not have the coloring of its parents until it is five or six years old.

Andean Condor *(Vultur gryphus),*
Young Adult; of South America

## PREY

Most vultures live on carrion. In Africa, the lappet-faced vulture *(Torgos tracheliotus)* is often the first vulture to feed. The huge lappet-faced vulture can tear open the hide of even a dead elephant.

The Egyptian vulture *(Neophron percnopterus)* has a long, thin beak to pluck flesh from between bones. This vulture also eats eggs. It uses its beak to pick up and throw stones at an egg until the shell cracks.

The bearded vulture doesn't throw anything. Instead, it often carries bones into the air and then drops them. When the bones break open, the bearded vulture feeds on the soft matter inside.

Black Vulture with
Dead Opposum

## VULTURES AND PEOPLE

People often fear vultures. They think of death when they see them.

Vultures are really harmless to people. In fact, vultures are very useful. By eating dead animals, vultures help rid nature of its garbage and disease. It is not surprising that vultures are protected by law in the United States.

Even laws haven't been able to help the endangered California condor. Scientists hope to raise enough condors in zoos so that one day these condors can be returned to freedom in the wild.

# GLOSSARY

**Birds of Prey** (BIRDS uhv pray)—birds which feed on other animals and have hooked beaks and talons

**Carrion** (KARY un)—the meat, or flesh, of dead animals

**Decay** (deh KAY)—the process by which flesh spoils

**Endangered** (en DANE jerd)—an animal which is in danger of being completely wiped out

**Prey** (PRAY)—an animal which is hunted for food by another animal

**Scavenger** (SKA ven jer)—an animal which feeds on dead animals

**Soar** (SORE)—to fly high with few flaps of the wings

**Species** (SPEE sheez)—within a group of closely related animals, such as vultures, one certain kind.

**Talons** (TAL ons)—long, hooked claws on the feet of birds of prey

# INDEX